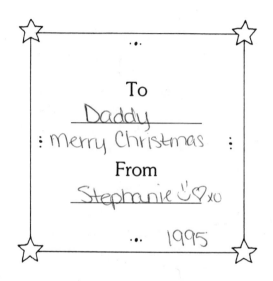

To

Daddy

: Merry Christmas :

From

Stephanie ☺♥xo

1995

Fathers Are Like Elephants Because They're the Biggest Ones Around

(But They Still Are Pretty Gentle Underneath)

Fathers Are Like Elephants Because They're the Biggest Ones Around

(But They Still Are Pretty Gentle Underneath)

David Heller

Villard Books New York 1993

All rights reserved under International and Pan-American
Copyright Conventions.
Published in the United States by Villard Books, a division of
Random House, Inc., New York, and simultaneously in
Canada by Random House of Canada Limited, Toronto.

Villard Books is a registered trademark of Random House, Inc.

Library of Congress Cataloging-in-Publication Data
Heller, David.
Fathers Are Like Elephants Because They're the Biggest Ones
Around / David Heller.
p.   cm.
ISBN 0-679-41758-3
1. Father and child.   2. Fathers and sons.   3. Fathers and
daughters.   4. Fatherhood.   I. Title.
HQ755.85.H45   1993
306.874'2—dc20   92-27269

Manufactured in the United States of America

3 5 7 9 8 6 4 2

To my father,
with love

Introduction

✩✩✩

One of the most compelling sayings about fatherhood is that "one father is worth more than a hundred schoolmasters" (George Herbert). Indeed, our fathers teach us so much. From overseeing our first childhood steps to offering advice to us as adults, fathers guide us and help us find our way in life. Conventionally, they teach us to ride a bike, swim the backstroke, or how to fix a flat tire, but their impact is emotional too. Fathers influence our view of the world and typically instill in us a sense of integrity and self-esteem.

This book is a tribute to fathers and to the role of fatherhood in modern life. It is also a celebration of the father-child relationship, which is unsung as a formative force but is no less powerful than a mother's relationship to her offspring. Like mothers, fathers are dedicated to our happiness and well-being. Even though their challenges and sources of stress may differ, fathers are there for us too.

What follows is a collection of humor and wisdom about fathers and sons and fathers and daughters, and a lively portrayal of fathering itself, all through the eyes of little experts who have much to say about their own fathers. The children turn the tables on us and provide some memorable banter about such subjects as: what all fathers have in common, typical things that fathers say, the many things that fathers teach you, the popularity of sports among fathers, and what to write in a winning Father's Day card.

The young people are playful with their fathers, but they evidence much respect and affection as well. While they share many insightful observations about fatherhood in general, child after child will convince you that there's nobody else quite like their own dear ol' dad.

—DAVID HELLER, PH.D.

Fathers Are Like Elephants Because They're the Biggest Ones Around

(But They Still Are Pretty Gentle Underneath)

Thoughts About the Nature of Fatherhood

☆☆☆
☆

"They make good buddies except for that
discipline stuff."
Quentin, age 10

"Fathers are like elephants because they are slow
movers and they're the biggest ones around, but
they still are pretty gentle underneath."
Cynthia, age 9

"Fatherhood gives you gray hair, but some of those men look better that way."
Laura, age 8

"Not all fathers have a hood. My father only has a father hood when it's raining out."
Ben, age 6

"Fatherhood isn't for weaklings, but it's not for macho nuts either."
Geoff, age 10

"Fatherhood is awesome if you like to eat the macaroni that your kids don't finish."
Len, age 8

"My dad is good at fatherhood, but he isn't finished
with it yet. . . . I have to grow for
a lot more years first."

Gene, age 7

"Fathers are like bagels—kinda hard and crusty on
the outside but soft on the inside . . . and they're
always around in the morning too."

Julie, age 10

What Is a Father For?

"Fathers are for barbecuing in the summer."
Marie, age 9

"You play sports with them and you teach *them*
some of the finer points of the games."
Arnold, age 10

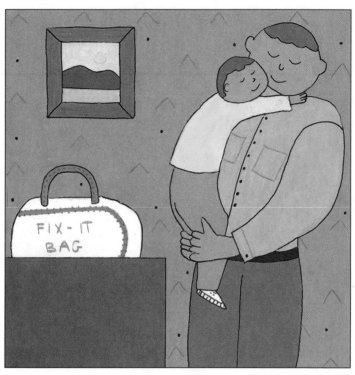

"Fathers are for fixing things . . . like bikes and when you get your feelings hurt."
Larry, age 8

"They buy you the expensive sneakers that your mother wouldn't buy for you."

Tim, age 8

"Fathers are for picking daisies with you, but only when the other fathers aren't looking."

Joanne, age 7

"The number one thing that fathers are for is loving."

Erica, age 7

Glimpses of What Prehistoric Fathers Were Like

☆☆☆

"The first ones were darned scared because they had no idea what their children would put them through."

Robert, age 9

"Adam wasn't rude like some of the fathers are now, like the fathers that watch car chases on TV all the time."

Alexia, age 8

"Those fathers were half nice and half rough. I don't think they were big on giving stuffed animals to their children, though, because they might have known that type of animal personally."

Arnold, age 10

"They were like giants, and they demanded that their food be there on time. . . . exactly the same as it is now."

Margo, age 7

"Since they didn't have cars yet, the fathers just washed their stones and spears during the hot summer days."

Carlton, age 9

"Prehistoric fathers worked for the dinosaurs, and when they got home, they complained that the dinosaurs were idiots and that they didn't know how to run a business."
John, age 10

What Do All Fathers Have in Common?

"All fathers put their feet on their table."
Suzy, age 7

"They are just boys who like to tease the women they love."
Alexia, age 8

"Every one of them I ever met liked playin' poker."
Albert, age 9

"They take you to hockey games and basketball
games, and they teach you to yell at the players."
Reid, age 10

"They all kiss their kids on the way to work, and
we kiss them back if they remembered to shave. . . .
If they didn't, it's too scrubby and we just
tug on their ties."
Kelsey, age 7

On How Someone Qualifies to Be a Father

☆☆☆☆☆

"To be a father, you have to have a deep voice and you have to practice growling."

Robbie, age 8

"You have to know a lady pretty good first, and then it's good if you marry her and then you can be a father just like that."

Pat, age 7

"Fathers wear big, itchy sweaters that almost hide their
stomachs, but not altogether."
Janice, age 8

"There's no test or nuthin'. . . . You just have
to know about what kids eat and what sports
to teach them."

Sean, age 8

"I think you have to be at least eighteen. . . . It might
be thirty in some states."

Michelle, age 8

"There's no special way you can prove you
are ready to be a father. . . . You kind of get
on-the-job training."

Terry, age 9

"A lot of them have beards and mustaches, but they
don't make you grow one just to be a father. . . .
You get to choose it yourself."

Toni, age 6

What a School for Dads Would Be Like

"It would be something like army camp, and the dads would be all out of breath."
Robbie, age 8

"The school would be a fun place with swimming pools and basketball courts and video games, and the fathers would have to take a crash course in all of them so they will know how to play with their children."
Michael, age 9

"They would have special classes on how to change baby diapers, and most of the fathers would get a note from their fathers excusing them from class."

Sharon, age 9

"The teachers would show the fathers how to clean out the cat litter."

P. J., age 6

"The fathers would learn how to talk to children and how to listen to them. Most of the fathers would be good at it, but a few of them would have to go for extra help."

Terry, age 9

"Fathers teach you that the game isn't over until you see two
O's on the big time clock."
Liz, age 6

The Many Things That Fathers Teach Their Children

"They teach you to use a handkerchief when you
sneeze, even if they rub it on their
sleeves themselves."
Nicholas, age 7

"You can learn all the inside stuff about
Ping-Pong from them."
Tim, age 8

"Fathers teach you the hard way not to let them give you a haircut. . . . Pay the money and go to the barber."

Frank, age 9

"Sometimes they teach you to swim. They make you believe you're like a fish. I like to play like I'm a shark and my brother is a little fish in the water."

Matt, age 6

"My father likes magic a lot, and he's a lawyer too, so he teaches me a lot of tricks."

Carey, age 7

Common Fatherisms
(Paternal Sayings)

" 'Fee-fi-fo-fum . . . food, food, food . . .
I want some!' "
Jamie, age 9

" 'I know it's hard for you, but try to be a gentleman
. . . and stop pulling your sister's hair!' "
Albert, age 9

" 'You don't need that toy. Let's be a wise young man and save for your college education.' "

Frank, age 9

" 'Promise me that you won't tell your mother that I broke that dish.' "

Dana, age 8

" 'What's on television tonight, sport? Something *I* like?' "

Quinn, age 7

" 'Do the best you can at whatever you do . . . and don't pay any attention to those corny friends of yours. . . . They're illiterates!' "

Jack, age 9

"Fathers are for reading stories to you and skipping
the scary parts."
Krista, age 7

What Kind of Man Makes the Best Father?

"A millionaire kind of man who is also very generous
with children."
Lauren, age 10

"The best kind is the father that will watch
cartoons with you."
Joy, age 6

"A tall man makes the best father because he can reach the badminton set if it's on top in the closet."

Dionne, age 7

"Chubby men make good fathers because they are fun to hug and they know what foods taste the best."

Molly, age 7

"The fathers that are good at teaching things. My father is the best teacher. . . . He taught me how to saw and how to build a tree house, and he even taught me how to keep out the rain."

Randall, age 9

On What Dad Was Like Before He Became a Father

"According to my grandmother, he was a pain
in the rear."
Bea, age 8

"I think he just read *Time* magazine and waited until
the right girl came along."
John, age 10

"He wore old corduroy pants with patches, but then my mother converted him."
Mimi, age 9

"He used to be pretty wild. Once he even went skydiving. . . . He must have been some kind of nut!"
Arnold, age 10

"He was a handsome son of a gun . . . just like me!"
Jack, age 9

What Does Your Father Look Like?

☆☆☆☆☆

"Do you mean before work or after work? . . .
He looks different dependin' on which
you're asking about."

Patrick, age 8

"My daddy is very good-looking. That's what my mother says. . . . I'm not supposed to be able to tell the difference yet."

Jane, age 6

"He looks something like me except he has bigger hands and feet."

George, age 6

"You can pick him out real easy. He wears a watch."
Dee, age 5

What Do You Like Best About Your Father?

"Personally, I like the way he loves children."
Michael, age 9

"My dad has a lot of old warm shirts, and they make good nightgowns for me."
Liz, age 6

"I admire how much my father loves my mother. . . .
My husband better treat me like that or I'm going
to beat him up."

Laura, age 8

"The best thing about my father is that he is friendly
and every person likes him except for the people in
my family—we love the guy."

John, age 10

Dad's Favorite Things

"He sure loves his golf clubs. . . . I don't know why
because they don't do him much good. I caddie for
him sometimes. When I do, I always wear old
sneakers because I know I'm going to get a
lot of sand in them."

Joe, age 10

"My father likes our pool the best, because he likes to do belly flops and show his belly."

Eddie, age 6

"When there is a race on TV, he acts like he's a race car driver, and he makes noises like *zoom* and *varoom!*"

Jason, age 5

"My dad likes hammers. . . . That's all I can think of."

Ben, age 6

"My dad likes his glasses a lot. He thinks they make him look smart. It don't matter when I'm around, though, because I always hide them so he can't do any work, and he has to play with me."

Willie, age 7

"His favorite thing is cable TV. That way he can watch
four games at a time. I guess I don't have as big
of an attention span."
Arnold, age 10

Eccentric or Downright Weird Things About Selected Dads

"He has long conversations with our dog."

Alexia, age 8

"If he sits too long at the kitchen table, he starts to sweat and get sick . . . because he can't go long without being in the same room as the TV."

Laura, age 8

"I never once saw him sneeze. I don't know what he does to get unstuffed."
Jerry, age 6

"There's nothing weird about my dad. He's a man's man. That's why we call him Chief."
Andy, age 9

"He likes to walk around in his underwear, but I thought that was kind of against the law."
Nelson, age 8

"The weirdest thing about my father is that he reads all the time and he never watches television. He must be the only person in America who doesn't."
Charlotte, age 8

Ways to Get a Dad to Slow Down If He's Working Too Hard

"Tell your father to tell his boss that he has the father's flu."
Albert, age 9

"You could call him at work and make up a story, such as your mother ran away with another man."
Rebecca, age 8

"I just tell him: 'Daddy, take a break,' and then he sits down immediately and says, 'Yes, ma'am.' "
Shari, age 9

"Make a chocolate fudge sundae, but tell him he has to take a break if he wants to eat it."
Robbie, age 8

"Force your father to chase you around the block, and then he'll get tired and slow down."
Dick, age 7

"If you say that there's a swimsuit contest on television, then your father might take a break."
Laura, age 8

"My dad has big muscles and a big heart too."
Marie, age 9

On the Popularity of Sports Among Many Fathers

"It's just something they're born liking. Even when they're just little and crawling around, they always try to fight for the ball."

Juliet, age 8

"My father doesn't really like sports that much. I think he just watches to drive my mother nuts."

Ellis, age 9

"Fathers like to imagine that they're the ones playing, instead of the players. Fathers are childish. They should be playin' with their daughters and tellin' us how pretty we are."

Charlotte, age 8

"My father knows who all the players are. He's kind of a genius."

Steve, age 8

"Sports is like life, man. . . . It beats going to the opera or the grocery store."

Jim, age 10

"They can escape from their jobs and wish they were the ones making five million dollars instead of that Clemens stiff."

Arnold, age 10

How Good an Athlete
Is Your Father?

☆☆☆☆☆

"My dad is excellent at plumbing. He gets a real
workout when he does it."
Alexia, age 8

"I would like to see my dad wrestle Randy 'Macho
Man' Savage. He could give that dummy a
lickin'. . . . But my dad doesn't have any time. He's
too busy because he's an accountant."
Dale, age 8

"My father's favorite sport is drinking gallons of Pepsi. . . . He's gotta have it."

Bea, age 8

"I went to his softball games. He can hit the ball far. But he still didn't get the ball to where the people with the gloves are. . . . He should try harder."

Stacy, age 5

"He isn't good like the Chicago Bulls are, but he is the kind of basketball player that will let you win sometimes."

Eric, age 9

"He's an okay athlete, but he's great because he's always there to play catch with his children. . . . I think fathers were created so there is always somebody to play catch with."

Joe, age 9

About Fathers, Their Cars, and Their Driving

"They like to show off and do those U-turns, but me and my brother always close our *eyes* when he does it."
Dick, age 7

"My father loves his van. He always wants a new one. My mother would like to have a new child every year. So they make a compromise. . . . They get a new cat every year because that's cheaper than either one."

Laura, age 8

"He sure would love a fast sports car, but the money is going to a special place that is going to help pay for my college. . . . He loves me more than any car."

Gloria, age 9

"All fathers think that they're twenty years old. They should be more like women when it comes to cars. . . . We're dignified!"

Charlene, age 10

When Dad Is the Chef

☆☆☆
☆

"He makes ugly stuff like hard red beans."
Sean, age 8

"The food he makes tastes funny and bumpy. He's
usually watching a baseball game and he forgets
that the timer is on."
Albert, age 9

"My father is a real burner . . . even toast."
Rebecca, age 8

"My dad taught me everything he knows about making birthday cakes. . . . He calls himself Billy Crocker."

Marie, age 9

"When he cooks dinner, he puts too much hot spices in it. . . . My mouth hurts on the inside for a long time after."

Jill, age 7

Original Father's Day Cards

Dear Dad,
How are you doing, baby? Guess what? I'm alive.
Elvis
Ed, age 10

To Daddy,
You shouldn't have punished me for not
listening yesterday.
No Father's Day present for you, Jack.
Your very mad daughter,
Krista, age 7

To Pop,
I hope that you are not still sore that I won that bet
on the Super Bowl against you.
You got to use your head when you bet.
Happy Pop's Day,
Arnold, age 10

Dear Dad,
You are a neat dad and a lot of fun. I wouldn't trade
you in for any other dad except maybe one that
makes a million dollars.
Love,
Robbie, age 8

Dear Father,
I just wanted to tell you that I love you even though
it's hard to say. I almost start crying when I think
about it, because I feel so much. Have a
happy Father's Day.
Love,
Cynthia, age 9

Concerning How Fathers Really Feel About Love

"My father thinks love is fun and interesting. . . .
He's the gooey explorer type."
Lannie, age 7

"They give you a lot of love when they come home
at night, and they don't ask for anything in
return—just maybe a kiss on the cheek and the real
truth about what happened at school."
Maria, age 8

"They are big on love if the mothers are the ones doing all the work around the house."
Bart, age 9

"I never ask him personal things like that. . . . I just ask him about turtles and snakes."
Dee, age 5

"My dad must like love, because he gets a magazine that he keeps in his drawer that is all about it."
Laura, age 8

What Every Father Needs to Know in Order to Get Along with Children

"You have to know how to tie your kids' shoes in case your kid doesn't know how yet."

Ben, age 5

"If you can play the guitar, that can make up for something else . . . like if you're not so good at building tree houses."

Keith, age 8

"You have to know how to put together about
seventy different toys."
Charles, age 8

"Fathers should be able to whistle with their fingers. Then they can teach important things like that to their young ones."

Les, age 8

"You need to remember that you should spend as much time as you can with your children, because pretty sooner or later, they are going to be all grown up and you will be too old to run races against them."

Leigh, age 8

Do Fathers Treat Sons and Daughters Differently?

☆☆☆☆☆

"No. They'll go on a water slide with either one."
Krista, age 7

"Fathers treat sons better because they got
something in common . . . big egos."
Sharon, age 9

"They treat us all like little jewels, and we're all real
valuable to them."
Myra, age 8

"As long as the kid is tall, the father will play a lot of hoops with the kid . . . boy or girl, black or white, smart or dumb, it don't matter."

Deion, age 8

"If either a boy or a daughter talks back to the father, either one is doomed. There's no difference."

Maria, age 8

"Sometimes they're easier on girls. But they're tough on my kind because we remind them of when they were little boys. But they forget that we got computers and technology now so we're plenty more grown up than they were."

Albert, age 9

On Children Imitating
Their Fathers

"I sure would like to copy how much money he
makes, plus I have to admit that he's funny
sometimes . . . well, once in a while."
Tim, age 8

"I like to go where he goes. . . . We're like a team."
Brian, age 7

"Most kids are different than their fathers. The fathers weigh two hundred pounds and the kids are lucky if they're eighty. You got to eat milkshakes all the time to catch up."

Howard, age 8

"My father is a class act, and that's how I got to be one too."

Michael, age 9

"Girls don't copy their fathers. . . . Why would we want to be pigs around the house?"

Alexia, age 8

On Why Some Fathers Are Called Teddy Bears

"Fathers are like toy teddy bears because they need batteries or something else to get them going."
Charles, age 8

"Some fathers have hair on them, and most of the bears I have seen do too."
Charlene B., age 7

"They call them if they're big fans of the football team from Chicago and their coach, Mike Discus. . . . Actually, he looks like a bear."
Keith, age 8

"People call the men teddy bears just to get them embarrassed."
Alexia, age 8

"My father isn't a teddy bear. He is more like a moose!"
Dick, age 7

"My father is like a teddy bear at Christmastime. . . . The rest of the year he is just a hardworking human being. But I still love him just the same."
Carter, age 8

What Are Fathers Famous For?

"Giving kids a hundred bucks and telling the kids to
have fun with it."
Tobin, age 10

"They're famous in a not so good way for smoking
cigars and warning you about smoking cigarettes."
John, age 10

"Fathers are famous for climbing mountains, or at least climbing up on your roof and gettin' your ball out of the gutter up there."

Ginny, age 8

"Fathers are known for taking their children to the park on Saturdays."

Krista, age 7

"Fathers are known for being tall and strong, and mothers are famous for helping them believe that they are."

Terry, age 9

"Fathers are famous for being the breadwinners. . . . In my family, we make sure he is also a cake winner and an ice cream winner."
Arnold, age 10

"Fathers are known for being sweet even though they are shy about it."

Myra, age 8

"Taking you to Cub Scouts and making paper airplanes with you."

Carey, age 7

Concerning Who Might Be the World's Most Influential Father

"The father of the guy who invented the car. He probably taught his son to be a mechanic, but he never expected such big results."

Rebecca, age 8

"The man who owns the NFL could be the answer, because he gets all the other fathers to watch his league on Sundays."

Mark, age 8

"Jesus's father sure has a lot of power."

Krista, age 7

"The biggest influence could be the father of Michael Jordan, because everybody is copying his child. . . . He probably just tries to make sure that all this attention doesn't go to Michael's head."

Barry, age 9

"The fathers of the guys who run for president have a lot of influence. They probably hope that their kid gets elected so that they can move into the big house with them."

Gordie, age 8

Do Fathers Really Know Best?

"Nah. . . . He always gets lost on the turnpike when he can't find the right exit."

Rebecca, age 8

"Nope. . . . He orders the dog to go to the bathroom on the newspapers, but our dog always goes right on his slippers."

Albert, age 9

"Fathers know best about how to throw a football
and how to fix a car . . . but mothers got them beat
on some other things, such as looking pretty
and making soup."
Sean, age 8

"It's a split decision between fathers and mothers
on who knows best."
Geoff, age 10

"Fathers haven't changed. They are pretty much like
walking encyclopedias you can count on."
Howard, age 8

"Even if they don't know best all the time, you
shouldn't yell at them because you might
hurt their feelings."
Sara, age 6

Why Do We Call It Father Time?

☆☆☆☆☆

"Because fathers never sit still and
neither does time."
Renee, age 10

"Because fathers control the TV clicker no matter
what time it is."
Charles, age 8

"It's called that because you can tell how good a father is by how much time he spends with his children."

Sean, age 8

"It's called Father Time because a clock has to use both hands to get the job done, and so does my father. . . . He's a builder."

Vanessa, age 10

"Because the person who was responsible for you being born—your father—is your father every single minute of your life."

Michael, age 9

"God was the first father and He made time . . .
unless we got it wrong about God. Then it should be
called Mother Time."

Elizabeth, age 9

Concerning What a Man Would Be Missing Out on If He Doesn't Get the Chance to Be a Father

"Wild vacations in Florida with your kids!"
Laura, age 8

"Father's Day cards every year."
Krista, age 7

"You might miss out on all that time where you just lay around on the couch and watch TV and get your children to keep getting you potato chips."
Bart, age 9

"You would not be able to have heart-to-heart talks with superintelligent people called children."
Michael, age 9

"In the winter, you would have to eat chili all by yourself. . . . That would be sad and lonely."
Lloyd, age 9

"You wouldn't ever have a reason to play with toys again."
Marissa, age 6

Why Fathers Are the Most Important People in the World

"They are the most important when they love their
sons or daughters with their whole heart."

Laura, age 8

"They pay for you to go to baseball camp. . . . Your
whole sports future could be at stake."

Robbie, age 8

"Fathers are the most important because they always
say yes even when your mother says no."
Shari, age 9

"You need a father. They can up your allowance."
Krista, age 7

"Fathers love you, and they help you feel like
a dynamite kid."
Geoff, age 10

A dad is a kid's best friend."
John, age 10

ABOUT THE AUTHOR

DAVID HELLER is widely known for his popular books about how children perceive the world and experience spirituality. He graduated from Harvard University and holds a Ph.D. in psychology from the University of Michigan. His work has appeared on ABC's *20/20* and in *People, Good Housekeeping, Psychology Today,* and *USA Today.*